SARAH BEENY

A Detailed Biography

John Brooklyn

Table of Contents

L et's engage in a casual conversation about the captivating life story of Sarah Beeny and explore her intriguing world. Born on January 9, 1972, in Reading, England, Sarah Beeny has made a name for herself in the realms of real estate development and television. Her unique blend of sincerity and humour has captivated audiences for decades.

Sarah has always been a hard worker, willing to put in long hours and take calculated risks. From selling vacuum cleaners door-to-door as a young girl to establishing her own real estate development company, Tepilo, she has consistently shown determination and ambition. Through popular series like *Property Ladder* and *Help! My House is Falling Down*, she has become a household name in Britain.

Sarah skillfully combines her enthusiasm, expertise, and practical tips to create an engaging show that inspires viewers to embark on their own home renovation projects. Prepare to be inspired and moved by the extraordinary journey of this remarkable woman.

SMALL BEGINNINGS

Beeny's childhood may have been unconventional, but she maintained a middle-class appearance with her stylish blonde streaked hair and trendy Ray-Ban spectacles. Brought into the world on January 9, 1972, by Ann and Richard, in Reading, Berkshire, she was raised with a solid foundation in the real estate industry.

Growing up, she spent a significant part of her youth in a caravan, living a life reminiscent of the fictional *Good Life,* tending to goats, ducks, and hens. The Beeny family called a nine-acre property on the outskirts of the Duke of Wellington's estate at Stratfield Saye in Hampshire their home, leading a lifestyle that Beeny humorously described as a bit like The Good Life.

Beeny and her older brother, Diccon, were enrolled in a boarding school following the unfortunate passing of their mother at the age of 39 due to cancer. Beeny attended Luckley-Oakfield School, an all-girls institution in Wokingham, on a weekly boarding basis to receive her formal education. However, she found herself feeling miserable during this period as she struggled with self-doubt about her appearance and felt like she didn't fit in with her female peers.

While her classmates pursued higher education, Beeny made a bold decision to follow her passion for theatre. Encouraged by her English instructor and fueled by her success in landing the lead role in Brecht's "*Caucasian Chalk Circle,*" she resolved to pursue a career in the performing arts. Beeny then enrolled at Queen Mary's College in Basingstoke, with the sole purpose of becoming a professional actor. She chose to major in theatre, dedicating herself to honing her craft.

Unfortunately, Beeny faced a setback when she was not accepted into any theatre schools. Despite this disappointment, she remained determined to forge her own path in the world.

Beeny embodies the independent spirit that characterizes many students in boarding schools. However, It is intriguing to ponder whether these struggles played a role in her decision to start a family at a young age and establish a company dedicated to helping others find their dream homes.. Her father, Richard, instilled in her a strong work ethic that propelled her through various menial tasks until she eventually found her calling as a real estate developer. He aimed to instill in her a robust work ethic, pushing her to engage in physical duties such as construction, cleaning, and clearing. There was never a moment to relax, as there was always something demanding her attention around the house.

The 17-year-old Reading-born decided to embark on a remarkable circumnavigation of the globe. Sadly, her journey was fraught with loneliness and seasickness. Despite these challenges, she eventually found her way back to the United Kingdom, where she embarked on a diverse range of occupations. From window cleaning to selling Hoover cleaners door to door, Beeny's determination knew no bounds. In fact, she even ventured into the realm of entrepreneurship by establishing her very own sandwich company.

Driven by an unwavering desire to be her own boss, Beeny dedicated her weekends to immersing herself in the intricacies of the real estate industry. Her thirst for knowledge and ambition to forge her own path were consistent. It was during this time that Beeny, alongside her brother and husband, made the audacious decision to establish their own real estate development company. Remarkably, they managed to save up a deposit and enter the industry without any prior experience.

Besides the real estate industry, Sarah's developed enthusiasm in connecting people together and it served as a catalyst for her and her friend, Amanda Christie, to embark on an exciting venture - the creation of a unique dating website called *mysinglegirlfriend.com*. In order to bring this innovative platform to life, they both made the bold decision to secure mortgages on their homes.

With the UK-based dating website, *Mysinglefriend.com*, Sarah and Amanda sought to revolutionize the online dating experience. Unlike traditional platforms, their website stood out by allowing users' friends to craft their dating profiles, eliminating the awkwardness and inconvenience of self-promotion. With an impressive subscriber base of over 200,000 individuals, the site adopted a refreshingly straightforward approach to matchmaking.

Before any content written by a friend goes public, the user has the final say, ensuring complete control over their profile. Additionally, friends have the power to invite new users to join the site, further expanding its reach. It is worth noting that My Single Friend Limited, a corporation based in England, successfully registered the domain name in August 2004.

Notably, the driving force behind this remarkable venture is the dynamic duo of

Graham Swift, Sarah Beeny's husband, and Sarah herself. Together, they hold the majority stake in this thriving business, propelling it towards continued success and growth.

Meanwhile, users of online dating services in the UK have been advocating for the criminalization of catfishing due to the severe psychological harm it inflicts on its victims. While catfishing is currently not illegal, *MySingleFriend.com,* a platform dedicated to helping its members find love and happiness, has taken proactive measures to combat this issue. They have introduced a new feature that evaluates all new profiles through an automated system and subsequently reviews them by human customer service representatives before making them public. Profiles that do not adhere to the platform's guidelines are either marked for further review or deleted entirely.

To enhance user experience, *MySingleFriend.com* allows users to request and display up to ten suggestions from their friends on the site. Although catfishing itself is not illegal, engaging in associated illegal activities such as fraud or the dissemination of hate speech may lead to legal consequences. Recognizing the importance of privacy, the platform has implemented improved privacy controls, granting users greater control over who can view their images.

MySingleFriend.com has also built a reputation as a warm and inclusive community, fostering an environment where users can forge new friendships.

In 2011, the website was listed for a staggering £15 million. Sarah Beeny, along with Telecom Express, a technology business, enlisted the services of the esteemed accounting firm BDO to manage the sale of their jointly founded company. As the online dating industry flourished, competitors swiftly presented initial offers ranging from £10 million to £15 million, while private equity groups also expressed potential interest. Nevertheless, the fate of the website remains uncertain, leaving us in the dark as to whether it was sold or if its original owners still retain control.

Beeny's Story

IN THE REALM OF PROPERTY

Beeny was approached to do a screen test for a leading role in a new television series on property development after meeting Sarah Delafield-Cook's sister-in-law at a hen party. The success of *Property Ladder* led to the creation of several similar shows, including *Britain's Best Home*, *Streets Ahead*, and *Property Snakes and Ladders*.

Property Ladder, a British television series, made its debut in 2001 and continued until 2009. The show followed inexperienced real estate developers as they purchased properties, often in need of repair, renovated them, and then sold them for a profit, a practice commonly known as flipping. The show's main appeal lies in the challenges and setbacks faced by these aspiring developers. In some cases, they seek the guidance of professional property developers to overcome obstacles and achieve success.

The program initially premiered on Channel 4 and was produced by *Talkback Thames*. It was subsequently broadcast on various networks, including *Discovery Real Time*. Beeny, a skilled property developer, featured prominently in the show, often depicted as either pregnant or not pregnant. In 2004, the format of the show underwent a significant change, with each episode showcasing two new developments instead of just one. This alteration was prompted by the increasing risks faced by creators in a declining market. Consequently, in 2009, the show was rebranded as *Property Snakes & Ladders.* Regrettably, this particular episode marked the final instalment of the series.

The Lifestyle Channel in Australia also aired episodes of the show. To maintain its viewership, The Lifestyle Channel decided to keep broadcasting the program under its original name, *Property Ladder*, even after it was renamed *Property Snakes & Ladders* in Australia. They didn't hesitate to keep the original title sequence intact.

In 2012, Beeny hosted a show called *Double Your House for Half the Money*, where she returned to the familiar format of following two sets of homeowners as they renovated their own houses instead of flipping them for profit.

Sarah's *One Year to Pay Off Your Mortgage*, a television series, was initially aired in 2006. Accompanying the show were several books and a weekly column authored by Beeny for the *Mail on Sunday*. In 2007, she engaged in a thrilling race against Jason Plato on the Channel 5 driving programme *Fifth Gear,* where they manoeuvred articulated lorries. Notably, during an episode of *The F-Word,* Beeny graciously allowed Gordon Ramsay's sheep to graze in her garden.

In August 2010, she took on the role of host for the Channel 4 show *Help! My House is Falling Down,* which was later renamed *House Rescue.* Displaying her passion for restoration, Beeny embarked on the renovation of *Rise Hall,* a remarkable Grade II-listed medieval home located in Rise, East Riding of Yorkshire. Her vision was to transform it into a stunning wedding venue. In November 2010, Channel 4 aired *Beeny's Restoration Nightmare,* showcasing her journey with Rise Hall. In a significant move in 2019, Beeny transferred ownership of Rise Hall to a prestigious event, weddings, and catering company. Her remarkable efforts were recognized and honoured by the Historic Houses Association/Sotheby's Restoration Awards.

Beeny's latest BBC One programme, *Village SOS*, premiered in August 2011. In this captivating series, viewers are taken on a journey alongside a passionate group of locals as they tirelessly strive to revive their community.

Her groundbreaking series, *Double Your House for Half the Money*, aired in 2012, offering a unique opportunity for those who had previously been unable to afford their dream home. The show served as a catalyst, inspiring homeowners to make small yet impactful changes that would significantly increase their property's value. Many homeowners embark on the journey of purchasing affordable houses with the intention of renovating and upgrading them. However, unforeseen challenges often arise, leaving them in need of Beeny and her expert crew to come to their rescue. Whether they have run out of funds or faced unexpected life expenses, Beeny's guidance becomes their saving grace. By following her expert advice, homeowners are able to double their living space without breaking the bank.

The first episode of this captivating three-season series begins with homeowners in shock as a portion of their beloved home crumbles before their eyes. Chaos ensues, and amidst the commotion, Beeny fearlessly takes charge at the heart of the action. This dramatic turn of events mirrors Beeny's own personal journey, adding an extra layer of intrigue and relatability to the show.

In the following year, Sarah expressed her disapproval of the UK government's *Help to Buy* program. This initiative was created to assist individuals in obtaining mortgages with a minimal 5% down payment and a mere 15%

guarantee. Sarah firmly believes that taxpayers should not subsidize homebuyers and supports why banks wouldn't insure risky loans themselves. She argued that there are already affordable houses available in areas with limited job opportunities, rendering the program ineffective in reducing housing costs.

Additionally, she asserts that constructing better schools should take precedence over revitalizing blighted neighbourhoods. Sarah proposed the idea of facilitating the construction of accessory housing units for parents or students, promoting intergenerational living. She believes this approach would alleviate strain on municipal services while benefiting children and their families. Sarah's strong opinions may make her appear as a potential political candidate, but she dismisses the idea with laughter. She prefers to take matters into her own hands rather than attend meetings. In a jesting manner, Sarah even suggests that being a tyrant would be amusing, despite her true aversion to such a role.

In 2014, Sarah Beeny delivered an engaging presentation titled *"How to Sell Your Home."* Three years later, she released *"How to Live Mortgage-Free with Sarah Beeny,"* an intriguing series where she converses with individuals from diverse backgrounds, delving into their experiences of achieving a mortgage-free lifestyle. This show followed a proven formula of transforming dilapidated shacks into habitable homes, but it specifically catered to those who yearn for a life unburdened by debt and exorbitant monthly payments. However, this aspiration often required participants to relinquish most of their possessions. Some resourceful individuals, lacking refrigerators, ingeniously found hiding spots for their food, such as beneath the floorboards. After six episodes, the series came to an end.

In 2018, Beeny introduced her podcast, *"At Home with Sarah Beeny,"* where she engages in intimate conversations with renowned personalities, delving into their personal lives and surroundings. Esteemed guests like Pearl Lowe, Tim Lovejoy, Lynn Bowles, and Jo Wood have all made appearances on the show, sharing their unique perspectives at different junctures.

Beeny made her return to television the subsequent year with an exciting new series on HGTV called *"Renovate, Don't Relocate."* This TV programme showcases Beeny's expertise as a real estate developer and renovations specialist, dedicated to helping couples and families of all sizes avoid the hassle of selling their homes and moving to a new location.

In *"Renovate, Don't Relocate,"* viewers are taken on a journey as Sarah revolutionizes interior design using innovative techniques such as full-scale floor plans and smart cameras. What sets her apart is her unique approach to problem-solving, where she delves into how people truly utilize their living spaces and devises creative solutions to enhance comfort without the need for additional square footage.

After an impressive run of 30 episodes, the show concluded in 2020, leaving audiences inspired and eager for more of Beeny's remarkable transformations.

After selling their London home and their wedding business at Rise Hall, the Beenys made the decision to relocate to a former 220-acre farm in Somerset. This move marked the beginning of their ambitious project: the construction of a low-carbon stately dream home for *Sarah Beeny's New Life in the Country*. While a new house had already been approved for construction on the farm, Beeny and Swift had grander plans in mind. They aimed to build a miniature mansion in a separate field, showcasing their vision and dedication to their new rural lifestyle.

The program not only delves into the construction process but also offers glimpses into Beeny's family life and her practical approach to rural living. Viewers are treated to heartwarming moments such as the birth of her dogs' adorable pups and the involvement of her teenage boys in household chores. As the show unfolds, we witness Beeny skillfully constructing combs for a beehive, all while her child grapples with a DIY project around the house. These intimate moments highlight the challenges and rewards of their new life in the countryside.

Interestingly, Sarah subtly hints in the first season that the relocation to Somerset was primarily her husband's idea. During a family glamping trip, a term coined to describe luxury camping fifteen years ago, it became evident that she is not entirely accustomed to country living. Sarah's preferences for sleeping arrangements and bathing rituals reveal her penchant for comfort, as she insists on a soft bed, ample pillows, running water, and a functioning toilet. Recognizing his wife's desires, Graham endeavoured to enhance Sarah's camping experience by adding some much-needed amenities.

In the second season, which premiered in November 2021, the couple completed the interior furnishing and decoration of their new house, while also making exterior upgrades such as restoring the hedges and planting trees.

During the first season, Beeny and his family faced criticism for keeping a wild rabbit that their cat had captured as a pet. Many viewers were outraged by their decision to keep a wild rabbit as a pet and their use of explosives to scare local animals. The idea of keeping a rabbit that the cat had brought in arose when their children suggested creating a mock Longleat petting zoo on their property. Several frustrated viewers took to Twitter to express their discontent. Eventually, the family decided to put up a birdhouse in one of their vast fields to attract local bird species.

However, following this, the family proceeded to hold their own fireworks display in the woods, much to the disappointment of onlookers. Sarah's neighbours expressed their disapproval upon learning about her plans for an expensive real estate development. The couple's planning permit and the protests from their Wincanton neighbours became the focal point of the first two episodes of the season. The proposed road access had garnered eight complaints from locals who were aware of the region's accident history and were concerned for their safety. The removal of hedgerows, which serve as vital connections between various habitats for numerous species also raised concerns. Consequently, due to public backlash, the proposed access point was abandoned.

Furthermore, there was a public outcry over the show's detachment from reality during the COVID-19 pandemic. Although the pilot was filmed prior to the outbreak, many viewers deemed its airing amidst the crisis as disrespectful and self-indulgent. They criticized the program for being unrealistic and questioned its decision to be broadcasted at all. However, there were others who supported the show, arguing that it provided a much-needed escape from reality during challenging times. As a result of the online discussions, a clear divide emerged between proponents and opponents. Despite the controversy, the property was still granted a building permit. April 2023 marked the start of airing for the third season.

Channel 4's *"Little House, Big Plans"* with Sarah Beeny made its debut in June of 2022. Following its success, Sarah Beeny's new show, *"New Country Lives,"* premiered on Channel 4 in May 2023. In this captivating series, Beeny accompanies urban dwellers as they leave behind their bustling lives and embrace a slower pace in the countryside.

Beeny's Story

BEENY'S WORLD

At the tender age of eighteen, Beeny's brother Diccon introduced the Reading-born to Graham Swift, who happened to be the brother of his spouse, Caroline. Little did Beeny know that Graham would eventually become her life partner and business collaborator. Initially, Beeny wasn't particularly thrilled about meeting her brother's girlfriend's brother.

However, fate had other plans. Surprisingly, just three months into their relationship, they took a bold step and purchased an apartment together, much to the dismay of Beeny's parents. Their commitment to each other grew rapidly, and within two weeks of dating, they decided to move in together. In 2003, only two years after establishing their own real estate development company, they tied the knot. Despite being married for two decades, they rarely use the four-letter 'L' word to express their affection for each other due to an inside joke from their early dating days.

The subject of their common joke revolves around the idea that people who say "I love you" too soon may have ulterior motives, aiming to entice the other person into sexual activities. Consequently, Sarah and her significant other prefer not to use these three words to express their feelings for one another. Over the years, they have grown accustomed to this arrangement. Sarah only gets to utter the 'abominable' three-letter word when expressing her love for her husband to their children. Intrigued by their parents' relationship, the kids have playfully questioned their father about his feelings for their mother, to which he wittily responds, "Yes, I love your mother very much." Sarah admits that she struggles to accept romantic gestures and would be at a loss for words if her spouse were to openly display his love for her.

Graham and Sarah, a couple passionate about cooking, enjoy preparing meals together. Graham takes charge of the kitchen during special occasions, aiming to impress, while Sarah handles the weeknight meals. As they savour a bottle of fine wine, their laughter fills the air, creating a warm and inviting ambience. On Sundays, Sarah encourages everyone to relax and sleep in, emphasizing the importance of taking it easy.

Sarah prides herself on being a forgiving and compassionate mother. She diligently enforces rules and expects her children to clean up their messes. However, her children often defy her authority and even suggest that she should impose consequences she can follow through.

Sarah's ultimate goal is to raise well-adjusted individuals who contribute positively to society. Therefore, she treats her children as equals in conversations, valuing their opinions and fostering open dialogue. Unfortunately, they ridiculed her when she suggested they explore a career in television.

The renowned real estate star revealed in a 2013 interview with *The Mirror* that she and her spouse frequently engaged in discussions about divorce during their children's early years. They experienced regular disagreements and occasionally resorted to using inappropriate language. However, Sarah realized that constantly mentioning divorce was needlessly causing anxiety in their kids, prompting her to put an end to it. Over time, the children became desensitized to the idea of divorce, as it no longer piqued their interest.

Despite fleeting thoughts of divorce, Sarah firmly believes that she will never leave Graham, as he is her unwavering support and she deeply loves him. She describes Graham as an exceptional spouse, possessing qualities such as handsomeness, talent, humour, and faithfulness. While Sarah playfully jokes about divorcing Graham, she acknowledges her profound reliance on him. He is her rock, always providing encouragement and support. Initially hesitant to accept Graham's assistance, Sarah eventually recognized his presence during her arduous battle against cancer.

Beeny's four sons - Billy, Charlie, Rafferty, and Laurie - are not only close friends but also talented musicians. Hailing from London, they formed a boy band called The *Entitled Sons*, which recently emerged victorious in the prestigious Pilton Stage Competition. This competition provides unsigned bands and solo artists from all genres across the UK with a chance to perform at the renowned Glastonbury Festival. Finally, on June 22, 2023, their dream became a reality as they took the stage at Glastonbury.

Graham, their father, has been an integral part of the band since its inception in 2022. Joining the band has not only allowed him to pursue his passion for music but has also brought him closer to his sons. Despite his self-deprecating humour about his limited skill set, jokingly claiming that his only talent lies in operating a van, Graham remains gainfully employed. He often finds himself as the target of playful banter within the band, but his tolerant nature and support makes him an invaluable member.

While their father's rock 'n' roll lifestyle may resemble a never-ending school experience, the band members continue to perform together at various festivals, including the illustrious Glastonbury. However, as time goes on, the boys inevitably venture into their own individual musical endeavours amidst the bustling music scene.

When the band brainstormed for a suitable name, they realized that people might assume they were privileged due to their appearances on their mother's TV show. To counter this misconception and establish their own unique identity, they coined the name *"The Entitled Sons."* Surprisingly, their mother wholeheartedly approved of this sarcastic moniker, recognizing their desire to carve out a distinct path separate from her own television fame.

"Break," the debut single by *The Entitled Sons*, was officially released on January 20, 2022. The song made its first live appearance in a local bar

and was even featured on the popular show, *"Sarah Beeny's New Life in the Country."* It didn't take long for the track to gain traction, quickly climbing the ranks and securing a spot in the top 10 on iTunes within a matter of days.

Following its initial success, *"Break"* reached its peak position at number 45 on the UK Singles Downloads Chart. Their second single, *"Unconditional"* which was released on March 25 centered around none other than Sarah Beeny herself. The album cover for *"Unconditional"* features a captivating blend of Sarah's visage with that of her son, Charlie. The red and white photo showcases Sarah's face on one half, while Charlie occupies the other, creating a visually striking image.

Upon hearing the awe-inspiring song for the first time, Sarah was overwhelmed with emotion and found herself moved to tears. On the contrary, when Sarah had the chance to listen to the lads practising their song, their noise became so bothersome that she couldn't help but slam the door and yell at them to quiet down.

The band released *"Not Invited"* as a single in April 2023. In May of the same year, they followed up with the release of *"It's Time."* Adding to their impressive lineup, the band released the charity song *"These Days"* on June 9, 2023, coinciding with the premiere of the *Sarah Beeny vs. Cancer* documentary. This heartfelt track is aimed to support Cancer Research UK.

The impact of their efforts was evident when, on June 16th, 2023, *"These Days"* entered the UK Singles Downloads Chart Top 100, reaching an impressive peak at number five. It's worth noting that the entire sales revenue from this single was generously donated to Cancer

Research UK, showcasing the band's commitment to making a difference.

Beeny's Boys present themselves with a remarkable blend of professionalism and self-awareness, effortlessly showcasing the fruits of their hard work. Their camaraderie is palpable, as they genuinely enjoy each other's company and foster a strong sense of teamwork. Moreover, they place great importance on addressing social concerns, using their platform to raise awareness and support charitable causes. It is also worth mentioning that the group's aesthetic and personality are deeply influenced by their mother, Sarah Beeny. This connection is evident in their shared values and the way they carry themselves, reflecting her influence on their artistic direction.

By 2020, Sarah began to question whether her sons were receiving a truly personalized education that catered to their individual needs.

She grew concerned that her eldest son was facing excessive pressure to succeed academically in high school. Recognizing her own limitations and her husband's artistic background, Sarah believed that her children would benefit from being surrounded by intellectually stimulating individuals. Consequently, she made the decision to enrol all four of her sons in a school located in the Glastonbury area.

The results were remarkable. Both of her children thrived in their new classes, with one of her older sons even winning the prestigious Junior Musician of the Year award. Additionally, both boys secured prominent roles in the school play, surprising Sarah as they had previously expressed dissatisfaction with their previous schools.

Meanwhile, Sarah fully comprehended the challenges of remote learning during the global pandemic. Despite witnessing the impressive advancements made by educators, she remains steadfast in her belief that traditional print materials still hold superiority over digital resources when it comes to imparting knowledge.

The presence of Beeny's brother and sister-in-law in Somerset played a role in the decision to move her family there. Despite not living under the same roof, their close-knit relationship and strong sense of community made it an appealing choice. Previously, Beeny's family resided in the Streatham neighbourhood. In 2001, when they were in their early thirties, the couple purchased *Rise Hall* in the East Riding of Yorkshire for £435,000, intending to make it their primary residence. However, in 2019, Beeny and Swift decided to part ways with Rise Hall, selling it for a staggering £1.4 million, and embarking on a new chapter in their lives by relocating from the bustling streets of London to the tranquil countryside of Somerset.

Dealing With Cancer

Beeny announced in August 2022 that she would undergo radiation and chemotherapy for cancer. Tragically, when Beeny was just 10 years old, her mother Ann, who had recently turned 39, succumbed to the same illness. In November 2022, *Channel 4* commissioned a documentary that delves into Beeny and her family's experience with her illness and its treatment. The documentary, titled *"Sarah Beeny vs. Cancer,"* premiered on *Channel 4* in June 2023. Throughout the film, Beeny discovers three lumps in her left breast, and viewers are taken on a journey alongside her as she undergoes diagnosis, treatment, and ultimately a mastectomy for her cancer. The story is presented with a unique blend of honesty and humour, offering a softer and less aggressive perspective than the title might suggest.

In a lighthearted moment, Beeny playfully replaces the clinical term "mastectomy" with the word "cushion" when referring to her own reconstructive surgery. She describes it as "stuffing a cushion... with memory foam," adding a touch of levity to an otherwise challenging situation.

Her husband, Graham, affectionately describes her as a force of nature, providing us with a glimpse into the experience of being by someone's side throughout their cancer treatment. With all four of their children now in their teenage years, they have become pillars of support for youngsters, helping them navigate the overwhelming stress of having a sick parent. Realizing her hair was falling out in clumps, she mustered the courage to ask her sons for help. In a touching gesture, her sons took it upon themselves to shave off her long locks, resulting in a poignant moment captured in a selfie where she held a handful of her own hair, accompanied by a caption expressing the unexpected challenges she faced. Afterwards, she sought assistance from the National Health Service (NHS) to acquire a wig as her hair began to thin due to the effects of cancer treatment.

In February 2023, as she returned to the hospital, her body adorned with 'tattoos' (markings for the surgery) acquired during her cancer treatment, she proudly showcased these marks of resilience. Both the Royal Marsden and Yeovil hospitals provided her with exceptional care, and she fearlessly posed for photographs, revealing her surgical markings before her most recent operation.

After Sarah lost her mother, she found herself in a perpetual state of anxiety. One of the most heart-wrenching scenes in the film showcases Sarah's emotional turmoil as she stumbles upon her mother's medical papers and engages in a poignant conversation with an oncologist. This encounter sheds light on how modern treatments could have potentially prolonged her mother's life, leaving Sarah grappling with a profound sense of loss and regret.

The film not only delves into Sarah's mother's past but also explores her own present, marked by her own battle with illness.

Driven by a desire to validate the effectiveness of her sophisticated treatment, Sarah embarks on a mission to prove to herself that it will indeed work. The revelation of her mother's treatment and the subsequent realization that vital information had been concealed from her exposes the pervasive misogyny prevalent in the medical profession during that time. For instance, Sarah's mother underwent chemotherapy that would have rendered her sterile, yet no one bothered to warn her about the potential consequences.

Initially, Beeny declined to have cameras present during her chemotherapy treatments, but she eventually relented. Throughout her journey, she showcased moments of resilience, where she felt relatively well after treatment, as well as instances of extreme sickness that necessitated hospitalization. In order to gain a clearer understanding of the size of the tumours, she underwent an ultrasound examination. The process of recovering from the mastectomy and reconstruction surgeries was a gradual one, requiring ample time. Beeny's candidness played a pivotal role in fostering a sense of unity and providing much-needed solace for others facing similar challenges.

Sarah's need for concealment served as the driving force behind the creation of this captivating documentary. However, she soon realized that by pursuing this path, she would only be burdening her sons with the weight of secrecy. In fact, she even contemplated withholding the test results from Graham, as she had not allowed him to accompany her to the appointment. Thereafter, she understood that keeping her children in the dark would inevitably lead to their suffering, prompting her to encourage them to openly share their stories with anyone willing to listen.

In Sarah's eyes, the detrimental effects of secrets became abundantly clear. Determined to break free from this destructive cycle, she made the bold decision to divulge the truth to everyone. Instead of opting for concealment, she embraced extreme transparency as her guiding principle. Initially, she shared her experiences through a thought-provoking magazine piece, and later, she fearlessly delved deeper into her journey through the creation of a powerful documentary.

At the conclusion of the video, Beeny offers words of hope to those battling cancer, emphasizing the encouraging rise in 40-year survival rates. She urges viewers to pay attention to their bodies and seek medical assistance if they experience any signs of illness. By sharing her own story, Beeny aims to alleviate the fears of others facing similar challenges. During her appearance on *ITV's This Morning*, Beeny encouraged viewers to promptly have any suspicious lumps examined, as doing so significantly improves the chances of a positive prognosis. In April 2023, Beeny joyfully announced that her doctors had given her the all-clear, eliminating her risk of cancer. However, she also expressed mixed feelings about the physicians' clearance and the ongoing therapy, which will involve medication for at least another two years and close monitoring.

TV show host Beeny has faced criticism on social media, but amidst the negativity, one of her viewers, a nurse, staunchly defends the merits of her show. The anonymous fan believes that her show serves as a much-needed escape from the harsh realities of life. In an era where distressing material floods the online world, she prefers to steer clear of such content.

Having developed a reputation for her unwavering optimism, Beeny possesses a unique ability to find the silver lining in any situation. She has learned to embrace her circumstances and is grateful for the ways in which they have shaped her. Interestingly, she ponders the idea that her life would have taken a different path had her mother not passed away, as she would have attended a different school. This contemplation leads her to believe that she and her husband Graham may not have found each other.

Advocacy

Beeny was one of 200 prominent individuals who signed a letter to *The Guardian* in 2014, urging Scots to vote against seceding from the United Kingdom in the September referendum. Sarah Beeny is a vocal advocate for research on brain tumours, which she believes does not receive adequate attention and funding. She emphasizes the significance of conducting extensive research to mitigate the devastating impact of this disease on human lives. Beeny envisions a future where cancer treatment is so effective that the notion of it being fatal becomes absurd. Additionally, she supports the organization Cardboard Citizens.

Facts

➢ Sarah has a strong aversion to goat cheese, regrets giving up playing the piano when she was younger, and secretly yearns to be the renowned ballerina, Darcey Bussell.

➢ Throughout her life, Sarah has always longed for a transformation. She defied conventions by being the first in her age group to wear a bra, which made her feel self-conscious about her appearance. She pleaded with her father for a boob reduction but he promised her that she'll undergo the transformation once she turned 21. Prior to meeting Graham, she never dared to wear T-shirts or any form-fitting clothing, but he encouraged her to embrace her body and start doing so.

➢ When asked about her most extravagant impulse purchase, Sarah revealed that she had spent £70,000 on seven acres of land in Dorset. Her intention was to create a camping haven for her children, as an escape from their cramped London basement. She stumbled upon this property through a broker and made a spontaneous decision to acquire it. For years, they enjoyed using it as a camping spot before eventually selling it at a profit when they relocated to the countryside.

➤ Currently, the family's sole asset is a dairy farm in Somerset, which they acquired for a substantial seven-figure sum.

Books

Sarah Beeny has written multiple books about the property market and making money, such as "Property Ladder: How to Make Pounds from Property", "Property Ladder: Profit from Property", and "Property Ladder: The Developers Bible". She has also written books on dating, including "A Date with Sarah Beeny: Mysinglefriend.com's Guide to Dating and Dumping, Flirting and Flings". Additionally, she has written a book called "Sarah Beeny's Price the Job" and "Property Ladder: Sarah Beeny's Design for Profit".

SUMMARY

Sarah Beeny, a renowned property management expert and English TV personality, hails from a creative and entrepreneurial background that has shaped her career at the intersection of these two fields.

Sarah's educational path took her to Luckley-Oakfield School, and she initially aspired to study theatre at Queen Mary's College. However, she faced rejection, which only fueled her determination to forge her own path. Undeterred, she embarked on a personal exploration of the world, taking on diverse jobs along the way. Her journey began with humble beginnings, as she worked various odd jobs to save up enough money to establish her own real estate development company. Eventually, her expertise and passion led her to become a host on *Channel 4,* where she presented captivating series centred around the industry.

Today, she shares her life and business ventures with her husband and business partner, Graham Swift, and together they have four sons.

Sarah's fame extends beyond her television appearances. She has gained recognition as the host of popular real estate shows such as *"Property Ladder"* and *"Sarah Beenys Selling Houses."* Additionally, she actively advocates for various causes close to her heart. With an estimated wealth of around $3 million, Sarah has also co-founded the dating service *MySingleFriend.*

Currently, Sarah resides in her picturesque country home, surrounded by her beautiful family. While she continues to film new episodes for her series, *"New Life in the Country,"* she remains committed to maintaining her health routine, ensuring a complete recovery and effective treatment.

Printed in Great Britain
by Amazon